DIÁLOGOS
BOOKS

...and the spring is veiled over

...*et se voile le printemps*

MOHAMED LOAKIRA

Translated by
Peter Thompson

Original Artwork by
Bouchta El Hayani

DIÁLOGOS
BOOKS
dialogosbooks.com

...and the spring is veiled over
an English translation of *...et se voile le printemps*
by Mohamed Loakira
Translated by Peter Thompson
Translation copyright © 2017 by Mohamed Loakira and Peter Thompson, and
Diálogos Books.
French original copyright © 2015 by Virgule Editions.

Printed in the U.S.A.
First Printing
10 9 8 7 6 5 4 3 2 1   18 19 20 21 22 23

Book design: Bill Lavender
Front cover and interior art:
Bouchta El Hayani, from the Virgule Edition.

Library of Congress Control Number: 2017962737
Loakira, Mohamed
and the spring is veiled over / Mohamed Loakira;
with Peter Thompson (translator)
p. cm.
ISBN: 978-1-944884-35-2 (pbk.)

DIÁLOGOS
BOOKS
dialogosbooks.com

ACKNOWLEDGMENTS

The translator is immensely grateful to Mohamed Loakira and Rachid Khaless for gracious support of this project, to the Roger Williams University Provost's Foundation for The Promotion of Scholarship and Teaching, and to the fulgor of Diálogos Books' mission.

A NOTE ON THE ENGLISH EDITION

This edition utilizes the front cover art and interior illustrations done by Bouchta El Hayani for the original French version from Virgule Editions. The interior pieces were in color in the original but are reproduced here in grayscale, and so will have lost some of their quality, for which we apologize. The original color drawings may be viewed on our website at dialogosbooks.com.

Foreword: A Trembling Veil

Can a poem (or a book—for this is a book-length poem) be topical and at the same time make you lose your bearings? Can it refer to current events and also entertain its own event—the unpredictable reactions in its own crucible? No mistake: Loakira's poem is about Arab Spring. But the power of his images shifts the reader from the uneasy Maghreb cities and onto another scene: the breaking and making, the revolts and improbable successes of poetry.

If you have lived through the tensions of Arab Spring, if your king has made adjustments (2011) to the Constitution—thus avoiding full-scale unrest—and if you've seen the insurgents and the café-bombs over the years, along with the repressions, how much do you owe to the *topic* (you the writer who deals with truth), and how much do you owe to the *poetry* that inheres in raw and visionary revolt? With Loakira both axes are operative, but the plain facts of Arab Spring act on us only to the extent that we are informed. His primary avenue to the truth of this era is instead metaphorical allusion—even while that allusion is crafted from the plain facts.

Here metaphor is the operation that de-centers the reader. Thus the reader who expects a clear lens on Arab Spring is asked to find a new center (or some kind of new middle) of meaning and emotion. This is a middle which is neither of the poles which spark metaphor between them. So if Loakira creates this perspective:

> *Neither am I that repulsive foaming, the whip,*
> *the sword, that sharpening tool*
> *aiming for the very flesh.*

it is a perspective that emerges from a series of negations, of things that are not quite, and that Loakira says "he" is not quite. Rather he is

> *Just a simple passerby, eager,*
> *hanging on by his very nerves.*
> *Detritus of a survival well-suited to my ravings.*

As with any metaphor, neither pole is as it's stated. Loakira is not the mindless firebrand or repressive torturer of the first lines, but neither is he "just a simple passerby." His "survival" and his "ravings" are his suspension in a state of betweenness, the aporia and reversals of mid-revolution. As with the outbreak of any revolution, its future is "veiled" (*voilé*). In another binary possibility, clear within the book's title, the betrayals and failures of Arab Spring mean that it is also "violated" (*violé*).

The many oppositions in this book keep us suspended as if we are groping for the meaning of events, but they inhabit a metaphorical architecture that eventually—as we finally sense what is being said *between* dueling assertions—forms coherence. The Moroccan writer and editor Rachid Khaless points out several oppositions. The book is lyrical, as he says, and so it is—an obvious *cri de coeur*. And yet Khaless values its "fundamental tone," which is its "link with the real." He points out (in his introduction to the Moroccan edition) that an "I" floats in the book, duels with "the world," but that this subjective/objective opposition finally blurs to a more disembodied "voice;" importantly, this voice is unable to assert what is real. He points out Loakira's glinting lucidity—but also (on the more lyrical side) his hallucinatory drunkenness (in his own words the poet is "drunk with immensity and mirages"). And that this is a "celebration," a "shadow trembling on the page"—but also that Loakira's style is essentially a "disconcerting economy."

As we've seen, Loakira's stance is a refusal to make one assertion about Arab Spring—to *see* what is real or to *know* what the violence means or will bring. There are a number of poetic elements in this "suspension," as suggested. But let's add another: to be aware of the uprisings under Abdul Karim (20th century) and the Emir Abdelkader (19th century), of the violence carried out by the present government in the Rif, and of all manner of other insurgencies in North Africa, and yet to stand with some poise in the Arab street in 2011 and spin this long tale of what is happening inside and outside of your head is to lean toward the metaphysical. It reminds us of Scheherazade's parlous inventions. It is like the wholly imagined insurrection in Abdelwahab Meddeb's *Talismano*, and the observer's refusal of *physical* action because "Our attack on history would only serve to further the notion of nation as the sole guarantor of legitimacy." It brushes against Meddeb's "There is nothing in which I do not see nothingness" (Jane Kuntz's translations). And it is a long tradition in the Arab world, back to Avicenna and beyond. A part (here, the poetic part) of the metaphysical tradition of examining a kind of moment of truth—the moment itself (but it's really the mystery) of artistic production. What, in my words (my invention), is *the real*, what is more true or more real than what I see before me?

The reader will deal in any number of ways with these harrowing propositions—as is fitting. The main goal here is simply to introduce this great contemporary (born 1945), present for the first time in English. Originally a Marrakeshi, he has been based in Rabat for more than forty years. One of the centers of the intense literary scene there, he has also held high government posts: Division Chief in the Ministry of Higher Education, and Director of Arts in the Ministry of Culture. His eighteen books have occasioned the highest awards, among them the Prix Grand Atlas (poetry) in 1995, and the Prix Grand Atlas (francophone novel) in 2010.

We should read the last few poems of the book with a special attention to link them. The upper case YA LILI YA 'AINI at the end of "while/obedient watchers" is a popular song.

—Peter Thompson

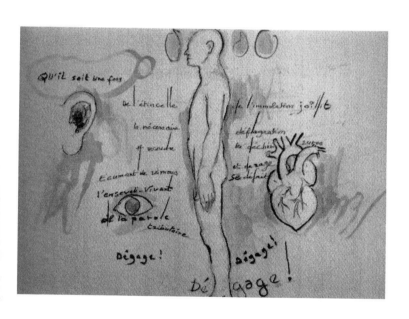

Qu'il soit une fois

de l'étincelle   de l'immolation jaillit

le nécessaire   déflagration
et accoudé   la fêchin
                                        et la rage
Écumant de remous   se défait
l'ensevel-Vivant
de la parole
tacaustaire

Dégage!   Dégage!

Dé) gage!

...and the spring is veiled over

...et se voile le printemps

MOHAMED LOAKIRA

Translated by

Peter Thompson

...et se voile le printemps

…and the spring is veiled over

Qu'il soit une fois.

May there be a once upon a time.

De l'envol des cendres de l'immolation,
dispersées hors-lisière,
étincelle la déflagration.
Eboulis de pierres fossilisées de sang,
de lambeaux de chair,
de filets s'embrasant en spirale,
chargés d'arômes enivrants,
s'en allant éclatés,

                              prolifèrent
tout près du lointain
Jasmin, musc, girofle ou cumin.

Que me cache la flamme migratoire
de la charrette calcinée ?
Et la ligne de mire m'invitant
à déployer les ailes dans un ciel tourmenté,
dépourvu de sillage ?

Out of the wafting of his ashes, his immolation,
scattered past the outskirts,
the spark of the explosion.
Rubble of stone, fossils of blood,
shreds of flesh,
strips spiraling in the flames,
heaving with intoxicating scents,
moving off after breaking up,

                         proliferate
hard against the far-off
Jasmine, musk, clove or cumin.

What is the transient flame
of the smoking hand-cart
hiding from me?
And now a sight-line inviting me
to spread my wings in a sky tormented,
a sky that's lost its wake.

Serait-ce l'aube naissante qui perce des nuages
teintée d'une brusque éclaircie aux larges éventails.
Rêve du possible, me semble-t-il, affranchi
et parcours remodelé à construire en partage?
Dirai-je, déclic furax empêtré dans le décalage
entre clarté soudaine et secrètes manœuvres?
Est-ce le jour qui s'apprête à annoncer
le début d'une nouvelle ère?
Surprenant réveil couvant l'étoile, matinale,
les pigments du soleil
ouvrant larges les territoires du souffle régénérant
l'ardeur?
Serait-ce cortège sans tête, compact,

                                hahaahaaaletant
après l'éclat désirable de la lumière, s'égare
au hasard de la fureur passagère?

Est-ce fausse-couche amère,
brouillon d'insomnies
ou simple fait divers?

Could this be dawn's birth, a cloud-piercing,
tinted by flashes at the wide transoms.
A dream of what's possible, so it seems, set free
and a route reshaped for sharing?
Might we say... a wan click, caught in the gap
between sudden light and secret manoeuver?
Is this the day, jumping forth to announce
the start of a new era?
Startling wake-up, hatching the morning star,
the sun's pigments
opening wide our lungs' territories and rekindling
warmth?
Could it be a procession without chief, compact,

                                        pa-pa-paaanting

for light's winsome ray, led astray
by random rage?

Might it be bitter miscarriage,
insomnia's rough-draft
or simply more of current events?

Ça fume.
A recoudre les blessures suffisamment légendaires.

Là-bas,
à l'inclinaison de là-bas qui rampe, s'étend, grossit,
partout se coule,
l'écho secoue ses vibrations, surgit,
se ramasse, s'étoffe, se répand ...
Coulée enflammée pétillante de bourgeons
Sinon déni des clins d'oeil en arrière.
Rejet des griffures, balafres, plaintes inassouvies,
lamentations de grand-mère.

Ouragan ou poudrière.
Plutôt éruption du volcan cru éteint.

L'oeil s'endurcit
Se vide des larmes aux abords de la compassion.

It gives off smoke.
Stitching the wounds sufficient unto legend.

Down there,
as the slope begins there, crawling, stretching, fattening,
everywhere a flowing,
the echo shakes off its vibration, rises up,
gathers itself, gorges, spreads…
A burning flow glinting with new buds
Or is it denial of any backward wink.
Rejection of claw-marks, gashes, unmet sighings,
grandmotherly lamentations.

Hurricane or power-mill.
More like an eruption, a volcano long thought extinct.

The eye hardens
Empties of tears on the brink of compassion.

Que le soleil se lève d'entre la grisaille de cet hiver.
Durablement inclément.
Qu'il abonde, horizontal, commun à tous les iris.
Réchauffant cimes, terre battue et bas-fonds.
Qu'il amplifie les cris du nouveau-né
mordant à belles dents le cordon et les tétons,
célébrant la fin de l'obscur dominant

qui, retardant

lever et éclat,

fait apparaître un semblant
de rayons disparates
se voulant apaisants.

Let the sun now rise out of this winter's gray.
Lastingly inclement.
May it abound, horizontal, common to every rainbow.
Warming summits, earthen floors and vacant lots.
May it fill out the newborn's cry
as he gnaws at umbilical and breast,
celebrating the end of the oppressing dark

                        which, holding back
                        sunrise and glow,

trots out a facsimile
made of motley rays
that try to seem calming.

Une lueur rebelle chatoie l'obscurité
qui,

  sous l'éteignoir,

  ignore son contraire.

Il est donc arrivé que le soleil voilé se soit défroqué
pour renaître du crépuscule.

Foudre bigarrée de lueurs ·

        (épurées ou cendrées)

d'où pendillent les étrennes du sacrifice
se drapant dans l'extrême urgence
d'imprégner de henné
la tresse ensanglantée.

A rebel glow makes the dark glimmer
which,

      under the candle-snuffer,

      knows not its opposite.
And so it happened that the veiled sun chose to be
    defrocked
to be born again out of twilight.
Lightning streaked with different glows

                   (purified or dusted with ash)
where the rewards of sacrifice dangle
draped in the extreme rush
to soak with henna
this bloodied tress.

Le sel et la chaux en incisures sur le visage,
l'enseveli-vivant
se défait de la parole
                    tributaire,
réclame une part de ce qu'il a rêvé.
Il s'attendrit,
                    échafaude, dévale
le déjà,
        l'en train,
                    l'advenant
                                qui s'étagent
sur les vestiges de l'incertain, des reports.

Ebullitions à l'entour du cratère.

The salt and lime, incisions on the face,
the man buried alive
strips off the dependent

                              word,
claws back part of what he has dreamed.
He grows tender,

                    scaffolds up, and then lets tumble
the already,

          the in-the-middle-of,

                    the about-to-be

                              that rise stacked
on the vestiges of the unsure, the postponements.

The boiling all around the crater.

... et la multitude vocifère, se serre
les épaules, les tendons,
                                    s'accroche
à la densité du cri aux confins
                            de l'exaspération,
va grandissant,
                    marche
sur la muraille penchée sur sa hauteur,
                                m'entraîne,
vague déferlante à travers
le rectiligne et l'angulaire,
au bon voisinage
d'autres voix (crues) libérées des larmes séculaires.
Même dissonantes, trouble-fête, obscures
Même sourdes aux timbres et tempos attenants
Chacun sur son chemin, faisant choix de mettre
en avant
tant les nécessités terre à terre
que les faveurs et promesses de l'ailleurs.

...and the multitude roars, hunches
its shoulders, tendons,

                                    hangs
on the outcry's mass at the edge

                                       of exasperation,
keeps growing,

                           stalks
on the city wall leaning from the heights,

                                       pulls me along,
a wave unfurling through
everything angular, rectilinear,
jostling close
with other voices (crude) freed from secular tears.
Dissonant even, spoilsport, obscure
Even deaf to the pitch and tempo of the voice at our side
Each of us on his path, making the choice to put
foremost
both down-to-earth necessities
and the favors and promises of elsewhere.

Les yeux pleins d'adhérence.
Le coeur battant au rythme de la colère.

Armé de carton, de hargne, de lance-pierre,
je m'arrondis suivant le tangage et le roulis,
louche du côté des visions fragmentaires,
                    du va-tout,
écumant des remous, de rage
telle cracheur de feu à l'orée de la terre brûlée.

Alourdi de peurs, d'imprévus, de mémoires
de ce que furent les acquis rétractés,
je broie du noir,
marche sur les braises,
bois de l'eau bouillante.
Je me fends la calvitie,
délire du haut des trous, des turbulences.
Gueulard battant le pavé
en rangs désordonnés,
je mâche le râle sous les coups des baïonnettes.
Mélopées et hématomes s'étayent.
Sang, sueur, bile, rougeurs se fondent.
J'entre en transe
et pousse un coup de gueule à la cantonade:
                    Dégage!
                         Dégage!
                              Dégage!

Eyes brimming with their grasp,
Heart pounding to anger's beat.

Armed with cardboard, resentment, slingshots,
I swell to fit the roll, the pitching,
squint at splintered visions,
                    of the great wager,
foaming with this upheaval, this rage,
like the fire-eater at the edge of the scorched wood.

Weighted down with fears, with the unforeseen, with
    memories
of those benefits withdrawn,
I macerate the dark,
walk on coals,
drink boiling water.
I crack open this baldness,
rave above pits, turbulences.
A loudmouth stomping the pavement
in careless ranks,
I chew the death-rattle under bayonet thrusts.
Melopoeias and bruises back each other up.
Blood, sweat, bile, blotches all run together.
I fall into a trance
and freely jaw the crowd:
        Out of the way!
                Out of the way!
                        Out of the way!

Que la fraîcheur de la cohésion !
L'inexprimable de l'enchantement!
Suaves, suaves attachements
au monde en constitution !

Ça empoigne l'avancée empreinte de démesure.
Poings dressés
Voix éraillées
Torses bombés
                    A découvert
Echauffourées, débandades
                              S'entrecroisent
                              S'entrelacent
                              Se font. Se défont
Reviennent. S'amassent. Se soudent
En dépit des bastonnades.

                    (Cours donc incorporer ton toi en moi
                         A ne plus être qu'un).

This cool breeze of belonging!
Ineffability of the spell!
Sweet, sweet bonds
with this world-in-the-making!

It seizes the vanguard, the footprint of excess.
Fists raised
Voices ragged
Chests thrust

                Out in the open
Skirmishes, routs

                              Criss cross
                              Interweave
                              Form. Come undone
Come back. Pile up. Meld
In spite of police clubs.

                (So run to fold your you into me
                      To no longer be just one).

...et le corps à califourchon sur corps,
fût-il taiseux, brimé,
délure, se démembre, endure, se casse
                                        la gueule,
ravale, se désagrège pour franchir les limites
                                        du corps
et trame le noeud d'une voie
en cours de balisage.

Ça brise le clinquant, le paraître,
occupe, arpente, dépave, incendie
places, guérites, sièges,
poubelles, artères ...

Ça brave menace, insultes, coups, traînages ...
Puis bivouaque,
s'accolade et partage
le cru de la soif, l'acharnement, l'intempérance.

...and one body astride another,
whether furtive, or bullied,
is wised up, comes apart, endures,

                              beats itself up,
swallows again, goes to pieces to cross the borders
                              of the body
and weaves the knots of a path-
way of signal lights.

This shatters the glitter, the appearances,
it takes over, measures out, pulls up pavement, sets alight
the squares, sentry-boxes, headquarters,
trashcans, throughways...

Braves threats, insults, blows, being dragged away...
Then it bivouacs,
embraces all and shares
the harvest of thirst, tenacity, intemperance.

Puis brouillage.

Divergences
des lignes à franchir, de l'entame du parcours.
Radicalement à rebours?
Ou parité et horizon à peine entrouvert?

Puis désaccord, rupture, séparation d'itinéraires

Puis poursuites, croisements de fer

Et sang coulant de part en part de la lame de fond.

(J'ai bien cru au miracle
à l'emballement du temps
au survol sous-estimant
l'ancrage de l'affront
sans donner du temps
au temps)

Then it blurs.

Divergings
lines to be crossed, at the first step of the journey.
Radically against the grain?
Or evenhandedness and horizon barely cracking open?

Then disagreement, rupture, forking of paths

Then chases, crossings of swords

And blood flowing through all the groundswell.

> *(And I really believed in the miracle*
> *in the soaring of time*
> *in its overflight yet underestimating*
> *this affront and its anchor*
> *not giving time*
> *enough time)*

Houleux, l'océan.

Déchaîné, le lac blanc
du juste milieu.

De bout en bout des rivages de la désolation.

Choppy, the ocean.
Raging, the white lake
of the happy medium.
From one end to the other, shores of desolation.

Et à part la vague qui me déroule,
m'échappe la pétulance du courant
en rade,
           à bon port,
                       faisant naufrage
des pêcheurs marins en détresse, des corsaires.

Debout ou à tâtons.
Ai-je écartelé l'élan du jet des pierres, postillons,
slogans, défis, aspirations (longtemps ravalées)
alors que la rive embrasée
glisse sous un ciel troublant,
se voilant subitement.

Ai-je adouci rêves, chemins de traverses, abîmes,
saillies ...
que j'ai escaladés,
d'où je me suis écroulé
                        Sans défaillir
                        Ni crier gare

And quite aside from that wave that lays me out,
the rip-tide's pull eludes me
while it wrecks,

in the roadstead,

safe in harbor,
fishermen in distress, corsairs too.

Upright or groping my way.
Can I have split the vital torrent of stones, postilions,
slogans, gauntlets, yearnings (long stifled)
while the flaming shore
slips beneath a roiling
and suddenly veiled sky.

Have I softened dreams, short-cuts, abysses,
outbursts...
that I once scaled,
only to tumble from

Without weakening
Or yelling Look out!

Maintenant
Dois-je me mentir et gober l'arrivée du printemps
en plein hiver ?
Me sacrifier au superlatif pour mériter
les ruisseaux du paradis promis au gratifié
qui s'écarte du proscrit,
dédaigne les jouissances d'ici-bas?

Ou céder aux injonctions et dérives des rigoristes
qui confisquent le *chant général*
                               à peine ébruité,
édictent le sens unique,
le révolu,
le partout-commettre-l'illicite
érigés en citadelle aux meurtrières hallucinatoires
qui escortent mes traversées,
me musèlent, me menacent,
me promettent l'intense
Flamme arracheuse des membres ...

Now
Must I lie to myself and wolf the dawn of this spring
while it's still winter?
Sacrifice myself to the superlative in order to deserve
the streams flowing down from paradise to the award-winner
who side-steps the forbidden,
scorns the hedonism of the here-and-now?

Or give in to the injunctions and side-drifts of the moralists
who confiscate the *general anthem*

                                   just beginning to spread,
pass edicts on the one-way-only,
the done-with,
the wrong-at-every-turn
built up as castles with hallucinatory arrowslits
that seem to escort my every crossing,
muzzle me, threaten me,
promise me the intense
Limb-ripping Flame...

Ou serais-je contraint à fonder l'outrance,
assassiner le rêve de renaître de mes espérances,
étreignant le futur à mains jointes ...

Ou arrondir le dos sous les gloses des prédicateurs
et autres exégètes
jusqu'à mâchonner le silence
alors que le sang coule des yeux du rêveur partageur ...

Ou attendre dans ma retraite
l'écho de la déflagration
et saupoudrer les saignées de sel affadi.

Il n'est que dépossessions, flagellations, amputations,
rapts, rançons,
que ravage, feu et sang.

Et que s'allonge la liste des hérésies!

Or am I forced to endow excess,
assassinate my hopes' dream of rebirth,
strangling the future with both hands…

Or bend my back under the glosses of preachers
and other exegetes
mutter only in my own silence
while blood flows from the eyes of the partisan dreamer…

Or await in my retiring
the echo of the explosion
and powder the bloodletting with salt that has lost its
    savor.

There is only unlawful taking, flagellations, amputations,
abductions, ransoms,
devastation, blood and fire.

And may the litany of heresies drone on!

La constance reforge la passion inaltérée
Remet à plus tard l'astreinte de l'abandon

C'est là qu'est l'île ombragée de mes évasions
Aura de lumière sur lumière
Ferveur, altruisme, voeux du coeur
Refuge du cheminement illuminé
Et nul besoin d'intermédiaire
Non redevable à aucun manipulateur.

Persistence reforges an unchangeable passion
Postpones being forced to withdraw

My island is there, the shaded isle of my evasions
Aura of light upon light
Fervor, altruism, the heart's vows
Refuge of the shining way forward
With no need for intermediaries
In debt to no deal-makers.

...ne suis qu'un chiffre pointé.

Sans suite ni virgule.

Point d'oeillères.

Autant sur la terre ferme que sur la nuée passagère.

Ni prêcheur dans le désert.

Vengeur de foi, détenteur de la vérité absolue.

Ni souffleur sur les cendres volantes.

Ni déterreur de cadavres, censeur, harceleur
de jeunettes à l'air du temps,
de noceurs,
d'égarés ordinaires.

Ni égorgeur de contradicteurs.

Non plus écume répulsive, fouet, sabre, aiguisoir
lacérant l'intime de la chair.

Simple passager assoiffé,
accroché aux derniers nerfs.

Rebut d'une survivance à l'avenant de mes folies.

...nothing but a number checked off.

With no decimal point, no places after...

No blinders on me.

Seated just as much on firm ground as on a passing cloud.

Nor preacher in the wilderness.

Holy warrior, nor keeper of the one truth.

Nor breather on ashes.

Nor unearther of cadavers, censor, harasser

of today's young women,

of revelers,

of run-of-the-mill lost souls.

Nor butcher of my adversaries...

Neither am I that repulsive foaming, the whip, the sword,
    that sharpening tool

aiming for the very flesh.

Just a simple passerby, eager,

hanging on by his very nerves.

Detritus of a survival well-suited to my ravings.

Tantôt reclus-couche-lève-tard-jouisseur
Leurré de tant de lueurs temporaires
Ivre d'immensité et de mirage
Par-delà le surnombre et le rien nécessaire
Adepte du vivre et laisser vivre
A sa guise
Récitant les versets, les psaumes ou les poèmes des maudits

Tantôt transi de peur d'être

(à mon insu)
embobiné au point de disposer ma tête
parmi d'autres têtes

(Vas-y coupeur de têtes !)
de grossir le cercle des réprouvés (à fond de cale),
ensorcelé par les divagations des affabulateurs
et l'excès des chauffeurs de salles.
Puis noctambule,
irai-je me recroqueviller
dans un corps désintégré,
pestiféré par tant de cruautés, de clivages, de salissures

(Lâcheté ou résignation ?
Sinon reflets, chocs, ébréchures
qui se confondent dans la pupille,
s'interpénètrent,
inversifs, éclatent
tel l'éclair.
Débris empilés dans le miroir aux alouettes)

Sometimes a recluse late-to-rise hedonist
Lured by all these passing glimmers
Drunk with vastness and mirage
Beyond excess and the bare necessities
Adept at the live-and-let-live
Each in his own way
Reciting scriptures, psalms or the poems of the damned

Sometimes stock-still with the fear of being
                              (not that I realize it)
fooled to the extent of setting my head
alongside the other heads
                    (Go for it, swing that axe!)
of joining the circle of reprobates (bilge-dwellers),
bewitched by the ramblings of tale-tellers
the exaggerations of the lounge-lizards.
Then nightstalker,
will I curl up
in a crumbling body,
plagued by so many cruelties, cleavings, sullyings

(Cowardice or resignation?
If not glints, shocks, chipping away
that swim together in the pupil,
interpenetrate,
spindle, burst
like lightning.
Debris piled up in the funhouse mirror)

Serait-ce le déluge ?

Ou le passage avant terme, éphémère

D'une cigogne solitaire

Perdue dans un ciel rouge-garance, menaçant?

Ou serait-ce le dénouement

De la dernière nuit

Des mille et une ?

So is this the Flood?
Or the passing before its time
Of a solitary crane, ephemeral,
Lost in a threatening, rose-madder sky?
Or could it be the dénouement
Of the last night
Of the thousand and one?

Il était une fois.

(Que de fois entonnée lors des veillées à travers
l'épaisseur des ténèbres, autour du braséro ou
sur les Places-berceaux du savoir,
sublimant lumières, sciences, maîtrise des mers,
errance des dunes, arabesque, boussole, chiffre
rond, force tolérant us, coutumes, provenances,
reyonnement, partage, feu hospitalier et traînes
cousues d'or, calligraphie droitière,
restaurant la foi
et célébrant la souveraineté du Suffisant-à-Soi
qui n'engendra ni ne fut engendré
et de qui n'est d'égal pas un . . .)

Once upon a time.

> *(Intoned so many times through long vigils*
> *through the depths of darkness, around the brazier*
> *or in the cradle of a people's knowledge,*
> *sublimating lights, sciences, mastery of the seas,*
> *dune-crossings, the arabesque, the compass, the round*
> *number, a force accepting all ways and customs, origins,*
> *radiance, sharing, welcoming firesides and dress-trains*
> *stitched with gold, calligraphy proper and adroit,*
> *restoring faith*
> *and celebrating his rule, the Sufficient-Unto-Himself*
> *who will father no one nor was he born*
> *and of whom there is no equal…)*

…or il est toujours l'hiver pesant qui perdure.
Du détroit au désert.

Il y a du pis-aller, brusqueries, parjures,
tromperies, débords, détours, failles.
Il y a des chu
        tes
fractures, saignements …
Il y a des relevailles.

Là, gît somnolente
l'ombre de Shahrayare-le-bicéphale
Vieillerie, os desséchés, végétant
au fond du vide-ordure

...and it is always this winter that weighs and endures.
From the narrows to the desert.

There are last resorts, abruptnesses, perjuries,
trickeries, overflowings, detours, fissures...
there are fa
                llings
fractures, bleeding...
There are recoveries.

There lies, dozing,
the shadow of Two-Headed Shahrayar
An old throw-away, parched bones, moldering
at the foot of a trash chute

Une tête tributaire de l'accidentel
accourt, s'époumone, mèche rebelle, coeur saignant,
expose à l' oeil nu le dissimulé de sa misère,
les couches épaisses de la rage ravalée,
se morfond de trop guetter la faveur de la lune,
pourrir sous le zinc, dans les égouts à ciel ouvert,
de trop languir du regard, trop assiéger les couloirs,
les croisées, issues, terriers bétonnés de considérants,
tendre la main, fouiller les poubelles, de trop d'envies,
trop
d'écarts, d'éclats ajournés, de récidives, d'impunités
et gavages des déjà-trop-engraissés,
déborde d'excès, d'urgence momentanés ...
                    (si par ras-le-bol le chaos détone),
ébauche les pointillés du monde entrevu entre autres
songes
gorgés d'outrage,
d'effroi ou d'exil.
Puis, à coups d'anesthésiants, aussi de serrages,
se rétrécit dans sa tanière,
tremblotant de retenues, de peurs,
de résignation en héritage.

One head, one that hangs on accident,
rushes up, howls itself hoarse, hair rent, heart oozing,
bares to every eye its long-hidden misery,
its massed layers of swallowed rage,
sulks, having so long stalked the favors of the moon,
rotted under tin roofs, in the open sewers,
having so long languished, staring, besieged the hallways,
the landings, the exits, the burrows stopped up by the ever-
            attentive,
having held a hand out, rummaged in trash barrels, moped
            its litany of wants,
and too many swervings, coups put off, repeat offences,
            impunities
and greasings of the already-well-fattened,
and now overflows with temporary urgency and excess…
                        (if, from exasperation, chaos breaks out),
sketches out the world's dotted lines glimpsed among other
dreams
steeped in outrage,
dread and exile.
Then, after anesthetizing blows, and all kinds of pressure,
shrinks back into its lair,
trembling from biting its tongue, from fears,
and the genetics of resignation.

L'autre tête,

        hautaine,

coiffée de luxuriance, insensible aux prières,

use de dureté, d'artifice, de supercheries,

le temps durant,

exhibe gigantisme, faste insolent, gâchis, accoutrement

de circonstance, solidité des reins et main de fer,

s'isole dans sa sphère,

grillagée de cerbères,

claironne du haut du perchoir les fondements de sa

        légitimité,

bercée de louanges, de menteries

et va ailleurs festoyer, jeter au hasard

dés, atouts, châteaux, yacht, ranchs, palaces, clubs

sous la congère,

se mettre au défi de cueillir les fruits interdits,

varier les douceurs,

corrompre postiches, croupes téméraires, chair

        immature ...

...et donner en offrande, à tout venant, l'essence de notre

sueur.

      (Comme si la marge s'identifiait avec tes

largesses)

The other head,

        haughty,

a truly magnificent hair-do, deaf to entreaties,

makes use of its hard edge, artifice, hoaxes,

for the time being,

reveals a kind of gigantism, an insolent luxury, debris, accoutrements

of the moment, a stiff back and an iron fist,

holes up within its sphere,

fenced by multi-headed Cerberus,

trumpets from its high perch the basis of its legitimacy,

cradled by every praise, every lie,

and then goes off to banquet, to freely scatter

dice, trump cards, châteaux, yachts, ranches, palaces, ski clubs

up in the snowdrifts,

to challenge itself to pick every forbidden fruit,

to vary their sweet temptations,

to corrupt the phony, the sassiest derrières, immature flesh…

…and make an offering, to one and all, of the very essence of our sweat.

(As if the marginalized could identify with your largesse)

Désagrégé, tu te meurs.
Un peu plus qu'hier.

Now apart, you are dying.
A little more than yesterday.

Moins que demain.

Tellement subjugué par l'emphase du verbe grisant
que tu renies paroles, serments,
tes propres accents et dissonances.

Dors, dors, mon moi duplicateur

Rallongeons donc (toi et moi) de concert
le pourtour de la coquille,
la résignation du Je asservi,
en biais à l'étincelle
en mal d'incandescence

Jusqu'à épuisement de la lenteur

Less than tomorrow.

So subdued by the bombast of the inebriating word
that you disown speech, pledges,
your own accents and dissonances.

Sleep, sleep my Doppel-Me

Then let us extend (you and I) as one
the circumference of the shell,
the resignation of I-bowed-down,
obliquely to the spark
that's missing its glow

Until slowness has run out

  pendant

que Shéhérazade en sursis
refaçonne le fard, le sautoir, la chevelure ...
s'écoute raconter, raconter et raconter
des contes ininterrompus
fabuleusement mensongers
pour endormir le sanguinaire
et perpétuer l'espoir de sauver les jugulaires...

  while

Scheherazade in her reprieve
fixes her make-up, string of beads, hair-do…
hears herself telling, and telling, and telling
the uninterrupted tales
so fabulously false
to lull a bloodthirsty man
and rekindle some hope of saving her veins…

pendant

que les veilleurs soumis,

néanmoins exaltés,

outrageusement dépensiers,

s'enflamment

sur les complaintes des phalanges,

des talons fendillés,

des flûtes, ciseaux, tambourins,

prenant la poudre pour fragrance printanière

et s'exclament

en contrebas de la lune blessée:

(YA LILI YA 'AINI)

                    while

obedient watchers,

exalted nonetheless,

and outrageously prodigal,

                    are stirred

by the plaint of aching fingers,

cracked heels,

flutes, percussion shears, tambourines,

taking gunpowder for some spring fragrance

                  and cry out

beneath a wounded moon:

               (YA LILI YA 'AINI)

Et la nuit s'intercale à la nuit.

And night interleaves with night.

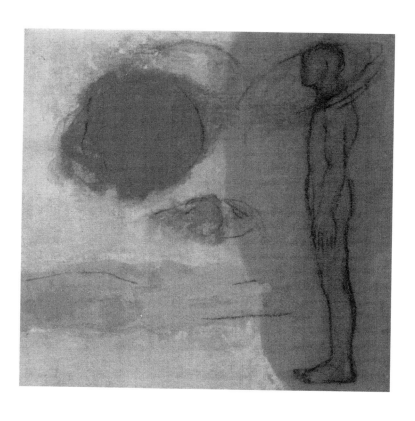

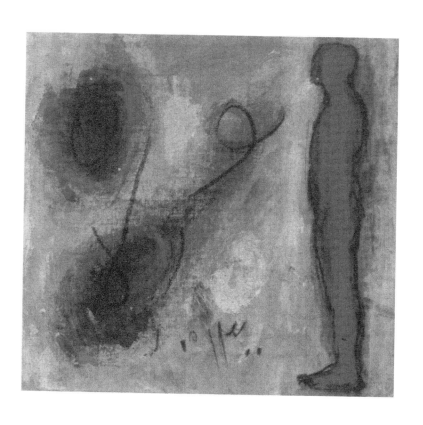

... et le semblant de l'aube apparaît
d'entre les contractions, le rebut des insomnies,
l'anesthésiant
et le brouillon des songes.
Longtemps attendu,
la voici si entachée d'abus, d'exclusions,
de cendres saignantes.
Peu attachante,
se faisant précéder de la sainte frayeur, du carnage,
ne se référant qu'à l'accomplissement d'autrefois.
Et moi de couver, d'affmer l'avancée à peine éclaircie
d'un rayon suspendu
                              à hauteur du contingent,
ce que fut exaltation,
et qui n'est que reculade empêtrée dans l'embrouillage.
Tanguant de l'oeil du soleil à la passion vers l'ailleurs.
Frappant à la paroi enflammée
qui s'étouffa d'impatience
                              d'où retentit encore
l'écho de l'exploit à la portée
d'une rare intensité.

...and something like the dawn appears
out of the contractions, insomnia's rejects,
the anesthesia
and rough draft of dreams.
Long awaited,
here it is, so stained with abuses, exclusions,
bloody ash.
Not really engaging,
only coming in after the holy terror, the carnage,
referring only to the exploits of the past.
It's for me to encourage, to refine the barely lighted coming
of a ray that hangs

               just at the height of the contingent,
what was once exaltation,
and is no more than tangled retreat caught in confusion.
Pitching and rolling, from the sun's eye to a passion for
    somewhere else.
Knocking on the flaming wall
a wall stifled with impatience

               and where the echo
of that feat within reach
of a rare intensity
still rings out.

Déjà là.
L'amertume de l'aube tardive défigurée ·
en cours d'apparition.

                    M'interpellant
Hé ! Passionné du vivre et laisser vivre
Allons donc attiser l'éclat d'une étincelle
La séparant
De la lave et des brisures séculaires.

Already there.
The bitterness of the belated and distorted dawn
as it just comes forth.

                    Calling to me
Hey! You, champion of the live-and-let-live,
Let's go stir up the glow of a spark
Prying it away
From the lava and centuries of rupture.

Délesté de ce que j'ai rêvé,
il m'arrive encore de remâcher
les débris de la mémoire du ressenti,
les Si, les Hélas du déçu
et la nostalgie de narrer l'exaltation.
Subite, puis détournée.
Du côté des psalmodies erronées.
Cachant la tête dans le sable mouvant.
Me claustré-je à l'abri
des outrances, coups d'épée, des flagellations,
dirai-je des balles perdues.
Alors que je fus ébloui
par les premiers rayons qui ensemencèrent
les repères de la nouvelle destinée, me convièrent
à talonner et remodeler la lumière.
Jaillissement et réverbères.
Audace, défi, aller de l'avant
et belles envolées d'une proche éclaircie.
Se recomposant, s'emballant, défroissant l'effroi
et enflammant le flottant.

Unburdened of what I dreamed,
I still end up brooding
over the debris of memory, of what was felt,
the Ifs, the Alas! of disappointment
and nostalgia for the tale of exaltation.
Sudden, but then turned away.
Toward the wrong-headed droning.
Hiding your head in quicksand.
Do I cloister myself in the shelter
of excesses, sword slashes, flagellations,
might I add stray bullets.
While I was dazzled
by the first rays that sowed
landmarks in a new destiny, and led me
to spur the light onward and reshape it.
Spilling forth of streetlamps.
Boldness, defiance, forging ahead
and the gorgeous fancies of the next sunny spell.
Remaking yourself, dashing off, softening fear
and lighting ablaze the streamers.

J'avais cru en ce que fut le début.

Espéré à répétition.

Et m'étais accoudé à l'espérant

                              en moi

                              se confiant

me semble-t-il, à ses dépits.

I had believed in what the beginning seemed to be.
Hoped for more of the same.
And leaned on the hopefulness

                              that confided

                              in me,

so it seems, to its chagrin.

Maintenant.

Les princes sans ascendance

s'arrogent désert, puits, rivages, holding, faubourg ...

déchiquètent

le souffle des assoiffés,

l'imprudence des passionnés,

rivalisent d'atrocités,

calcinant les vertes et les mûres

(comme si la barbarie était le signe distinctif de mon
*   appartenance)*

rackettent

décapitent

A l'ombre des appels consternés du minaret

Désapprouvant.

Now

Princes though lacking in ancestry
claim the desert, wells, shores, holding companies,
 neighborhoods...
and rend
the breath of those that thirst,
the rashness of those that have any passion,
rival each other in atrocity,
incinerating ripe and green alike
(as if barbarism were the mark of my belonging)
and racketeer
decapitate
In the shadow of disapproving calls from the minaret
Falling like frowns.

M'en vais-je, pataugeant
dans les renvois qui obturent les traces à peine esquissées
en regard de l'élan incontesté.
Gravats de cendre, sang, parti pris, captures, viols, bétail
concédé
au troc, servilité, déchéance humaine, violence fratricide,
horreurs,
exactions, supplications des punis de mort, craquelures
de l'entité,
de la diversité et conversion sous la torture
(qui n'est que diversion).
A mourir de haine et de lendemains vengeurs.

Perhaps I wander off, floundering
in the expulsions filling up barely-ventured tracks
in the matter of our uncontested soaring.
Rubble of ashes, blood, bias, seizures, rapes, livestock
handed over
for barter, servility, human decline, fratricidal violence,
horrors,
exactions, death row supplications, crazing of the surface
of the entity,
of diversity and conversion under torture
(which is only diversion).
To die from hate and avenging tomorrows.

J'abrège et me déclare insoumis.

Perché sur le vide.

Surmenant l'inabouti.

Mais résolu à ne pas cheminer

A reculons.

I'll cut it short and declare myself unbowed.
Perched over the abyss.
Overdoing the unfinished.
But resolved not to make my way

Backwards.

Books by Mohamed Loakira

- *L'horizon est d'argile*, poésie, Editions P. J. Oswald, Paris 1971.
- *Marrakech-Poème*, poésie, EMI, Tanger, 1975.
- *Chants superposés*, poésie, EMI, Tanger, 1977.
- *L'oeil ébréché*, poésie, Editions Stouky, Rabat, 1980.
- *Moments*, poésie, Editions Stouky, Rabat, 1981.
- *Semblable à la soif*, poésie, Al Asas, Rabat1986.
- *Grain de nul désert*, poésie, Editions Al Ittissal, Rabat, 1994. (Prix Grand-Atlas de la Poésie, 1995).
- *Marrakech: L'île mirage*, poésie, Al Asas, Rabat, 1997.
- *N'être*, poésie, Editions @ La Une, Rabat, 2002.
- *Contre-jour*, poésie, Editions Marsam, 2004.
- *L'esplanade des saints & Cie.*, récit, Editions Marsam, 2006.
- *A corps perdu*, récit, Editions Marsam, 2008.
- *L'inavouable*, récit, Editions Marsam, 2009. (Prix Grand-Atlas du roman, 2010).
- *Marrakech: L'île mirage*, folio d'art accompagné d'oeuvres du peintre Nabili, Editions Marsam, 2008.
- *Confidences d'automne*, poésie, Editions Marsam, 2011.
- *...et se voile le printemps*, poésie, Virgule Editions, 2015.